WE NEED TO TALK

Memoir and Essays:
The Road to Becoming an Ally

SHARON MOSLEY

Copyright © 2023 by Sharon Mosley

We Need to Talk
Memoir and Essays: The Road to Becoming an Ally

Print ISBN: 978-1-66789-649-6

eBook ISBN: 978-1-66789-803-2

Printed in the United States of America

TABLE OF CONTENTS

INTRODUCTION

I have hesitated to write about my experience up until now over concern that I may be, or may be seen as, trying to insert myself into the long overdue spotlight on systemic racism in our culture. How racism manifests is a part of my story, but I understand it does not equate to what it feels like to be a person of color living in a white dominated society. Mine is simply another viewpoint that casts light on the truth of the impact of racism.

My decision to write was partially inspired by a conversation I had with one of my grandchildren, a fourteen year old. When P was ten months old he came to live with my daughter, and she subsequently adopted him. J (Papa) entered their lives and also adopted him. P is a remarkable young man with many talents and interests, and he has autism. One thing very important to him is to study and understand the stories of people of various cultures. P is Black and indigenous Mexican.

One Sunday morning when he and I went out to breakfast, I asked him about what he had been doing that weekend. He told me he had watched a documentary on indigenous people.

Then in his recently discovered teenage mutter he said, "Not something you would know about." I replied, "Why do you say that?" He didn't want to tell me and said he didn't know. I told him I wanted him to tell me, and that I wouldn't be angry or upset. He finally said, "Because you are white." This was the first time he had brought up my whiteness to me, and I could tell he was uncomfortable, but was testing the waters. We proceeded to have a conversation about racial differences and about some of my experiences with people of various cultures, including Hawaiian culture from my fourteen years in Hawaii (which he was familiar with because he loved to visit me there). I told him that he probably understood more than me from his studies, but that I too appreciated learning about and respecting history and cultures different from mine.

I later mentioned this conversation to his mom. She said that my being white had come up from time to time, especially when he heard about things like police shootings and white supremacy. She told me she explained to him that some white people are allies, and Nana is an ally (one who associates with a person or group, providing assistance or support for their efforts). I was very touched and started to think more about what is an ally. In what ways am I considered an ally, and how did that process begin? I also realized how little my grandchildren know about my history and about my journey toward becoming an ally.

My intent is to write for myself, for my family and for any others who want to ask themselves any of the following questions: Would I like to become an ally? Am I working toward being an ally? What holds me back? What will help me? What supportive actions can I take?

I am sharing my perspective and experiences in this public way in the hopes that it will help us all to gain insight and understanding, perhaps revealing alternative ways of thinking about what we have previously believed to be true. This writing is for me a vulnerable place to relive the feelings of being misunderstood and rejected. My story is also one of love and acceptance in so many ways. I hope you readers will join me by reading with your personal mind and heart open to whatever glimpses of humanity you experience. You may wish to consider what we may understand now that those who came before us could not see or understand.

PART 1

MY PERSONAL PATH

CHAPTER 1

My story of learning how to determine what made sense to me and how to be my own person began somewhere inside of me in my youth, contrary to the heavy pressure for conformity from my mother and my environment. For much of my childhood and teen years I was a shy and compliant girl and student, but when I began to seriously question many of the conventions and assumptions of the time and place where I was born, I began a committed, and initially lonely, search for the life that was my own.

I was born in the South in a white conservative family and community, both of which were strongly Southern Baptist. My family was made up of honest, working class, church-going people who taught strict rules and values.

I grew up in the church, as did most of my extended family. The church had a strong influence on my taking seriously the rules of right and wrong and the desire to be a good girl. I was basically accepting of the rules until I was old enough to want to play cards with my friends and to convince my parents to let me go to school dances — two of the many prohibitions that a 13 year old girl couldn't appreciate. I began to see little value in most of the rules and to appreciate more the teachings of Jesus about compassion and how to treat people. I remained the shy, serious good girl, but I seemed to have a different way of seeing than most people I knew.

It was in my late teens when I confronted my first real conflict upon recognizing the hypocrisy that was ignored — the teachings not followed by the church-going adults. The greatest hypocrisy was the bias and treatment of Black people and the total segregation in our community. In my church and my home this was never spoken of. I knew what Jesus taught, and feeling and acting superior to those different from you did not fit! Although it was the Civil Rights era, in my southern town there was no sign of that. There was a Black population there, but I didn't know a single Black person. I became disillusioned and felt I had to find more like-minded people to relate to who would understand my interest in the Civil Rights Movement and the social justice causes of the 1960s, which I knew about from watching television news.

During my senior year in high school, on Christmas Day of 1964, my family was driving home from dinner at the home of my dad's family. I initiated a discussion with my parents, telling them that I needed to go to college. My mother's first response was "We thought you would go to secretarial school and get a good job at the plant where you could meet someone and get married." My dad shook his head in agreement. To my great relief, after some discussion, they said they would help me financially with college as much as they could.

After high school I got a job as a cashier at the neighborhood drug store where I had my first direct interactions with individuals who were not white. I started attending the local community college, and after two years I transferred to a university where I had two professors who taught me about the world outside the life I had experienced. Those teachings supported me in my need to question the status quo and speak up about what I felt strongly. They taught sociology and political science and spoke about current events such as demonstrations against the Viet Nam War, the Civil Rights Movement, poverty in our country, discrimination and the rights guaranteed by the Constitution and Declaration of Independence of our country.

Between my junior and senior years in college, I volunteered in a summer program that sent college students to various states to work in Vacation Bible School (VBS). This appealed to my interest in travel, new experiences and working with children. I was on a team with three students who came from Arkansas, Georgia and New Mexico. We spent about eight weeks moving from church to church in northern California. The young woman from Arkansas was African American and went to college at Arkansas AM&N, a historically Black college. She and I became friends. We shared much in common. We had a similar temperament, sense of humor and values. That relationship broadened my experience and my commitment to racial equality. This friendship influenced what came next —my first speech about segregation.

Upon returning home from that summer in 1968, the church my family and I attended asked me to give a talk on my experience teaching VBS in California. I was known then as a fairly bashful, pleasant girl, who would someday make a good Sunday School teacher. My mother was very pleased that I was asked to speak, and most of her church friends were there for that Sunday evening service. I was pretty new to public speaking, but I was moved to take advantage of the opportunity to speak about something that I felt strongly. Allyship (associating with a person or group and providing assistance or support for their efforts) was not a concept in my world or at that time, but there was a conviction to speak when I had the opportunity, not knowing if I would have any influence, be heard or be rejected.

I started with an overview of how we spent our days teaching and interacting with the kids, where we stayed, sights we had a chance to visit and the experience of working with a team of students from other states. Then I talked about my friend, JoAnn, and how I learned that color made no difference in friendship, working together or being roommates. I expressed my question about why so many still thought people should be separate based on color or other differences. Why was desegregation of schools taking so long? And why wouldn't churches, of all places, open their doors to everyone? All was quiet, and all I remember afterward was that all the congregates who spoke to me were polite ladies, offering no comments or opinions with one exception — one woman who simply said, "Thank you. That needed to be said". My mother said not one word to me about what I had said. Not that evening or ever. I was disappointed that it didn't open any doors for conversation, not even with my family, but I had no regrets. I felt I had done something valuable. I felt the truth of what I spoke.

CHAPTER 2

After college in 1969 I moved back to my hometown. I was ready to start looking for my place in the world during that era of dramatic social and cultural change. Like many of that generation, I wanted to live with purpose and make a difference in the world. I got a job as a social welfare worker. This job mostly involved interviewing and visiting people to determine their financial eligibility for assistance. It wasn't my idea of a job of social service, and my viewpoint didn't fit well in this workplace.

One of my first home visits was to an elderly woman in a rural area to determine her continued eligibility. "Were there changes in your income?" I asked. She proudly told me about earning a few extra dollars that month picking up pecans at her neighbor's farm. If I had written that down, those few dollars earned would be deducted the next month from her assistance check. That policy seemed cruel to me and contrary to creating an incentive to improve one's situation. I knew the job didn't fit my ideals and needs, but it paid the car payment and rent for awhile.

My displeasure with my work life was soon somewhat off-set by improvement in my personal and social life when I found a group of like-minded young people, something that I had sought for years. During this time many young people my age were joining the Peace Corps and other service organizations. VISTA (Volunteers in Service to America), the domestic version of Peace Corps, sent a group of volunteers from the east and west coasts to my hometown to work with Model Cities (economic development), welfare rights organizations and other "poverty programs" of that era. These "outsiders" were idealistic young people just out of college like me. As a local person, who met them with welcome and enthusiasm, I was an oddity to them, but I was warmly received into their small social circle.

That experience and the relationships that developed from that group fulfilled a deep yearning to connect with others who could understand me and who shared common ideals and pur-pose. Through that group I developed friendships with young Black people in my own hometown for the first time, because desegregation of the public schools that I attended did not begin until after I graduated high school.

I also discovered the small local church that was the spon-sor of the VISTA group . The church was attended by both Black and white local people, who I was thrilled to meet. I was happy to know that I was not the lone local. The minister was not local, but his messages resonated with my understanding.

CHAPTER 3

As I began to socialize with this group of young people, including several who were African American, I became the object of
a lot of gossip. There was distrust of these "outsiders," and a
local girl who would get involved with such a crowd must have a
major problem.

I had a party one weekend, inviting my new friends to my
new apartment. My guests included two African Americans —
one male and one female. The manager of the apartment com-
plex got upset by the racially mixed group and called the police.
The police came, but didn't seem to know what to do. I think
they warned us not to be too loud.

On the Monday morning following the party, my boss called
me into her office for some maternal advice. She told me she
got a call from my apartment manager about my having an integrated party. She warned me that I needed to stay out of trouble
and be careful about who I associated with. The extent of my
involvement with my new friends at that point was minimal. I

had visited the apartments of one or two of the VISTA workers, and hosted the one "infamous" party at my apartment.

She then, to my astonishment, warned me about gossip that was spreading about me. The rumors my boss shared left me aghast and somewhat amused. According to the calls she said she had received: I was sexually involved with a Black man; I was being treated for venereal disease by a doctor on the "far side of town"; and I was pregnant with a Black baby.

There was no basis for any of these tales, which seemed to be what someone thought were the worst things they could accuse me of. I was a bit horrified at how others had created a drama about my life. I suppose I was naive about the distortions and malicious tales people can create. It still seems like it was a dream rather than real. This drama left me a bit shaken by the extreme reaction to my association with two Black people at one party. After initially writing this I realized that it was not extreme compared to what had historically happened to Black men who were alleged to have looked at or talked to a white woman. Many did not survive.

My boss seemed perturbed that I was not taking what she was telling me seriously enough. Realizing her ineffectiveness at "straightening me out," she decided to have a couple of social work supervisors, who were closer to my age, talk to me. I gladly agreed, knowing these two men were not southern, thus believing I could express my point of view. She took me to their office, didn't say why I needed counseling and left me to tell them what this was about. I began to tell them why my boss thought I needed help. They were outraged! We ended up having a good conversation, and they were entirely supportive of me.

Dismayed about not having help changing my ways, my boss indicated that she knew I had a lot of compassion for "those people," but feared I was headed for trouble. She also must have felt obligated to call my mother to alert her. Needless to say, that began a very stressful situation for my family. They feared that I had lost my mind or come under some powerful, harmful influence. I know they sincerely cared about my safety and well-being, but they couldn't see that I was following my heart and values, and I couldn't follow their beliefs and norms on who I socialized with. They let me know they rejected me and how I was living my life. What I saw as being true to myself and values was a shock to them and an attack on their world.

CHAPTER 4

The eight VISTA workers occupied a small apartment building in downtown. I later became a regular visitor to their apartments and became especially good friends with Bruce and Gail from Los Angeles. I attended their parties and dinners, and soon got to know all of the group living there, including Ben, who was the local Black man who had attended my "infamous" integrated party. He was included, as was I, in the group's plan to take a holiday weekend trip to New Orleans.

There were eleven of us who hit the hot spots in the French Quarter and enjoyed the music and well known restaurants of New Orleans. We brought our sleeping bags and saved money by renting one room at the Hotel Monteleone. I believe that it was the first time any of us had been to New Orleans, and it was like a great escape to the Big City where we were not under the microscope of those who watched the "outsiders." It felt freeing and exciting to be beyond the frequent tension of my home town. A month or two later, I spent some time with Ben at a party at Bruce and Gail's. Shortly after that Ben and I began dating — something we had to keep secret, except from those in our immediate social circle. That meant mostly seeing each other at his place, our close friends' places or going out of town to see a movie.

It was rare that we went out driving in town, but one weekend we were driving on a major street, and I happened to notice that my parents were in the car behind us. We became very anxious and turned onto the first side street. I don't think they recognized us or the car, and they proceeded straight ahead. I knew they were headed to Gibson's Discount Center located on that street. (Gibson's was the forerunner of Price Club and Costco. It was the place to go on the weekend in many small southern cities.)

We learned to be very cautious. The fear of being confronted for being together was a real fear and something that kept us on edge. At some point my parents found out about our relationship. We learned this when one weekend, my dad showed up outside Ben's apartment when I was there. I never knew where he got the facts that led him there, but my car was parked outside. Obviously, someone had given him the apartment number. He banged on the door calling my name over and over. We stayed very quiet, fearful of what might happen if he got in. There was no way to see him or whether he might have a weapon. Although he owned hunting rifles, I didn't want to believe he would bring a weapon. Thankfully, he left after what seemed like an unbelievably long and anxious period.

This was followed by another encounter that Ben didn't immediately tell me about. He worked at an office only a couple of miles from my parents' home. One day my mother showed up at his office to tell him that he must stay away from her daughter. When he told me I didn't get a lot of detail, but I gathered that he just listened to her and avoided a loud confrontation in his workplace, and she left after she said what she needed to say.

I recall another situation that showed up in what was ordinary life for me, which illustrated the level of fear that could be triggered and how much I had to learn about what could be scary. I had a favorite place that I liked to go to get away. It was a rarely used, beautiful pine tree grove in a park outside of town. I knew that on weekdays there would be no one there. I thought it would be a romantic setting where we could be alone together. When we got there, Ben did not seem comfortable or at all impressed. He did not say much at first, but finally told me that he couldn't relax for imagining white men stepping out of the woods with guns, finding us together. That never occurred to me, but I could see why he would feel unable to relax and enjoy the peacefulness of this place as I did. (He didn't mention this as a factor, but he was a Viet Nam purple heart veteran, and he may have been also reminded of the war zone jungle.) We left immediately, and I felt I had learned a lesson about seeing from a different perspective in order to live in his world.

CHAPTER 5

The idea that I needed to get away and to have some time to think led me to decide that I wanted to join VISTA and go to another part of the country for awhile. The pressure from my family and my work and the understanding that I faced some big decisions about my life path influenced my need to be in a different place and to take some time with myself outside of the environment where I grew up. Also, there was still the desire to have a more meaningful job (working toward becoming an ally). I knew this would be a short term assignment, and I did not see it as a decision to leave the relationship. Ben seemed to support my decision, and he may have also felt we both needed time to consider the choices we had to make.

I completed the VISTA application and received an assignment to go to Philadelphia. I had never been to the East Coast. I packed up my car and left it in Ben's mother's carport with the plan that after I was settled, Ben would drive it to Philadelphia for a visit and then fly back.

I began several weeks of training with the VISTA program and became part of a team assigned to a community where we were housed with local families during the training period. I found that it was difficult for me to be as focused as I would ordinarily be or to feel settled there. I was distracted about my personal life and my decisions.

After Ben brought my car and spent the weekend, I felt even more unsettled. I began to feel that I wasn't going to be able to dedicate myself to the work there and that it was going to be really hard to be that far away from Ben. After some thought, I knew I was not ready to go back to my home town, but I needed not to be so far away. I called my friend, Jo Ann, (who I knew from our time in Northern California). She lived in a city about two hours drive from my hometown. I told her what was happening and that I was thinking of getting a job in her city. She said that I was welcome to stay with her and her sister until I found my own place. This seemed like a good solution. I left VISTA and drove back from the East Coast. I found a secretarial job and my own apartment within about two weeks, and I visited Ben or he visited me most weekends.

When we made the decision to get married after a year long relationship, we made the agreement to move to Northern California. We got married in the garden of a friend's apartment with Ben's parents and a group of supportive friends present.

A few weeks later we drove west and landed in Berkeley. Three of the former VISTA workers, who had concluded their work, had moved on to graduate school in Berkeley, and they welcomed us warmly. We had an immediate sense of community. It felt like home!

CHAPTER 6

We soon found an apartment just about a block off Telegraph Avenue and a few blocks from the UC Berkeley campus. Ben found a job with the City of Berkeley, and I found a secretarial job with a group of mathematicians who were planning college math curriculum.

We were excited to have found a new life with so much to explore in the Bay Area and a sense of acceptance as an interracial couple. Not feeling fearful to be in public together was a great gift. I felt comfortable in my marriage, the choices we made and the expanded world where we now belonged. I felt more free in myself and grateful that I was part of a world that was a better fit for me, living in a diverse environment of greater acceptance — a place where we could raise kids without the level of overt racism and obstacles that would limit their world and its opportunities, as would the world from which we came.

But as thrilled as we were to be living in an easier community, we did still live in the larger world where in some areas bias was more overt and recognizable, as we well knew. We were not blind to the fact that some degree of bias existed in any community, but the contrast we saw to where we came from was quite significant.

Being an interracial couple in 1971 was still subject to bias and stereotypes and feelings of being different. This was only four years after the U. S. Supreme Court ruled in an unanimous decision in Loving vs. Virginia that state laws banning interracial marriage were unconstitutional.

There are still stereotypes about interracial relationships, particularly about Black men and white women — the historically most feared relationship by whites, especially in the South. Perhaps, often unrecognized were, and maybe still are, the stereotypes about white women in relationships with Black men. I can name a few that you may or may not have heard: She's a slut; She can't get a white man; She has low self esteem; She identifies with being a victim. These ideas, of course, directly correlate with racist stereotypes about Black people. But I am not suggesting that it is equivalent to bias based on race. I am aware of the difference and the benefits that white privilege bestows. To name a couple: I can move through the world as a white person without being identified by most people by the color of my skin; Presumptions about me rarely have to do with skin color.

CHAPTER 7

After settling into our jobs and our new life of adventure we decided it was time to start a family. About a year and a half after our arrival in Berkeley, we became the parents of identical twin girls.

I became a stay at home mom, learning how to care for two babies. Needless to say that was challenging at times, especially without family nearby. But, of course, the joy outweighed every-thing else. Ben's mom came for two weeks to help out and fell in love with her first grandchildren.

During the girls' first year, we joined a mom and baby(s) group, which meant new friends for me and the girls. During my pregnancy I was in a Berkeley Women's Support Group, which provided much and continuing support. Fifty years later I still have close friends from that group.

While staying home after the girls were born, I decided that, instead of going back to work, I wanted to go to law school. I wanted to work in a public service legal career. I started law school in 1974, and the girls went to a small child care center near our house. Ben took care of the girls some evenings to give me study time.

While I was in law school, Ben and I divorced. Our differences were "irreconcilable," in the words of California law, due more to the lack of maturity and experience needed to be in relationship and not related to cultural or racial differences. We shared parenting the girls, and we both remain very involved in the lives of our daughters and grandchildren.

CHAPTER 8

When I finished law school, working with a children's services non-profit, I founded a legal project to support families with children being discriminated against in rental housing. We got it funded, and it served the cities of Berkeley and Oakland. It operated for several years until it merged with another housing discrimination organization in the area. I next became a Staff Attorney for the California Health Department until I retired.

After the girls finished college, and both began work as teachers, I moved to Maui, Hawaii for 14 years. I shared many wonderful Maui vacations during those years with my daughters and their families. We all, including four grandchildren, had very mixed feelings about my leaving Maui when I moved back to California in 2016. We live closer together now, but we all miss that special time together on Maui. Being closer, of course, means that I can be part of all the birthdays and special events, as well as, such things as simple as sharing meals, taking walks, and planting a garden with family. Gia/Nana (my grandmother names) feels very fortunate.

Returning to the San Francisco Bay Area, I moved to a senior housing community. In 2020 after the murder of George Floyd, I joined an advocacy group for diversity in the senior community. Many retirees came into the "streets" (sidewalks) to demonstrate for racial justice, against police violence and for actions and policies to support inclusion of more people of color in the housing community. It was uplifting to see so many elders participating passionately, making their voices heard.

This activity where I live and this period in May, 2020 that caught fire in our nation — a period of renewed demonstration, educating on police overuse of force, the need for updated police methods, the truth of systemic racism, and the broad presence of conscious and unconscious white supremacy — influenced me to think about what personal act of allyship I could do to speak to people about racial hatred and the state of our hearts. My grandchild's challenge and his mother's assurance about allies, as described in the Introduction, influenced me to do this writing, telling the story from another perspective — one that might speak to open, opening and openable hearts.

PART 2

Raising Children in a Racially Mixed Family

We are a nation of individuals of mixed origins — individuals of multiple cultures, races, ethnic identities and religions. There are pockets of homogeneous communities, but as a whole we are more mixed than we often recognize.

In this part I will be speaking particularly about my experience with biracial African-American/Caucasian children, who may face magnified issues about identity.

I'll begin with the commonly experienced challenge of hair differences. I wish someone had told me "Consult with someone who has hair similar to that of your children." I did my best without that advice, but I think my greatest weakness related to hair was not knowing anything about appropriate hair products. My daughters make no secret about the fact that their childhood could have been easier, if I had been more prepared to deal with their specific needs in this area. Some of you may think this is fairly insignificant, but I have learned that probably means you are not Black.

My daughters and grandchildren all have beautiful, natural hair, expertly managed, so I'm happy to say they are not currently suffering from my inept influence.

Diversity and multicultural living were present and valued in our life in Berkeley. The girls had friends and classmates from a variety of cultures. That was their norm when they began school. As they got older distinctions and differences began to be recognized and expressed by classmates, and their race consciousness began to grow.

The girls spent time with their dad regularly, and I believe both of us raised them not to consider racial distinctions as particularly significant. That was the ideal we held and the ideal we held for the world we saw as changing. In hindsight, I can see that we really didn't know how to prepare them for the real world they faced. I was pretty naive, and they were fairly unexpressive about the ways they felt different from both Black and white friends and classmates. They had mixed race friends and acquaintances, but from my perspective it wasn't until they entered college that they began to clearly experience the mixed racial identify as something to be discussed and explored.

They began this exploration by becoming part of a group of students who had mixed parentage. This group of college students recognized themselves as facing racial identity issues and sought the group support to express, rather than ignore, their personal and societal challenges. To some in the 1990's they represented hope, possibility, an ideal — an expression of true harmony. But knowing the history of the power imbalance of many racially mixed sexual unions as well as attitudes toward interracial marriage, they were challenged to discover themselves as members of a new racial frontier. At that stage my role was on the periphery. I could appreciate but not fully understand their experience. That's not totally dissimilar to being the mother of twins, which gives me some knowledge, but I cannot know the real experience of having a twin relationship.

My daughters grew up far away from their grandparents, both Black and white. In their early years they missed many of the benefits of extended family. Later, they had more opportunities to spend time with some members of Ben's family, as well as mine, which I will discuss more in Part 3. I do regret that they missed a greater involvement with family when they were young. I also wish I had understood the importance of their having more Black role models and exposure to more Black cultural events in their younger years.

Most of all I wish that conversations about racial differences, discrimination, identity, history and related feelings would have been easier in our home and would have started earlier. I think I thought their larger environment, schools and their diverse relationships were ideal and included all they needed at that time.

Despite what was missing in their education related to their identity, I have to give credit to their own pursuit of learning and understanding what they needed. Starting college opened a lot of doors that served them well, and they have continued to make any corrections that allow them to know how to fully teach their own children about their history and who they are. Their primary identity is proudly Black. They do not reject all of who they are or their extended family.

AN ASIDE: Just a few words about an inspiring son of an African father and white American mother. He became the 44th President of the United States. In "Dreams of My Father," Barack Obama describes with the most amazing clarity and candor his internal and external search for identity and understanding of himself. He grew up on the island of Oahu, Hawaii, living at times with his white grandparents. He appreciated the diverse community, but he had little contact with others from African descent. He eloquently tells of that palpable presence of racial tension that potentially presents at any instant for Black people, while he possesses and expresses the gift of an open and broad perspective, the apparent result of his thoughtful search for understanding.

The clear voice with which he tells his story made a deep impression on me because of the nonjudgmental way he presents the many characters and situations of his past. He describes the facts, the surrounding circumstances and the traits of the characters in his story with insight and respect. This seems to be the mark of deep respect for self and acceptance of others being

who they know to be.

PART 3

MY PATH WITH MY EXTENDED FAMILY

My choice to marry a Black man was the biggest action I took to step out of my family's world. I made numerous other choices that created distance: getting a college education; moving left politically; leaving the church questioning organized religion; leaving the region where I grew up; and becoming an attorney.

My parents must have felt rejected, hurt and probably confounded about how their simple world could have felt so overturned. I made my decisions without much discussion with them. I knew there wasn't really much room for discussion. I didn't see anyway to avoid hurting them, given their life views and how they differed from mine. I was hurt by their rejection, but to them I had choices and they thought they didn't.

After the move to California, I began to occasionally have phone conversations with my parents. For a long time they were unable to talk to me without asking "How could have done this to us?" I admit this was the reaction I expected. I never really considered the possibility that they could have done it differently. I wanted us to all move forward to acceptance, but I guess I wasn't certain that could ever happen.

When I told them I was pregnant and when I told them the twin girls were born, they were unable to say anything. When the girls were about six months old, Ben took them to see his parents. During that trip Ben's mom called my mother and asked her whether she wanted to see the babies. My mother agreed to go see them, and my dad drove her there. I was told my Mother went into the house to see them, and as she was leaving Ben's mom carried the girls out to the car to show my dad. My parents never spoke to me about that visit.

Later that year my dad died suddenly of a heart attack. I did not go to the funeral. A cousin called me just before the funeral. I had no reconciliation with my dad before his passing. But this opened a door for reconnecting with my mother. I talked to her about my coming to be with her after the funeral for awhile and to help her put things in order. She agreed and we both allowed acceptance to begin.

For a considerable period after my marriage most of my extended family had no contact with me. Remarkably, one uncle (the husband of my Dad's sister) and one cousin contacted me and let me know that they had not rejected me. On what was probably about my third visit to my mother, she made plans to visit my aunt at her farm where I went often as a child. They invited my

85 year old uncle, their brother, who I had seen on the previous trip. When we arrived, the wife of one of my cousins was there with a baby. We all chatted for a while and at some point the baby's mom put the baby on the floor to crawl. My uncle started trying to get the baby to crawl to him. He repeatedly kept saying "Come here n-word baby. Come here little n-word baby." I was completely shocked. He sounded like he was using the n-word as a term of endearment to a white baby. I didn't know what to make of it. I'd never heard the word used that way. No one said a word. Could he have been using it because I was there? Or was it common for him to use the word in that way, and he didn't even think about my reaction. I couldn't say anything. I didn't know what to say. He finally stopped, and no one ever mentioned it. I never wanted to think it was a passive-aggressive action. I knew him as a sweet man, who had been nice to me on our previous visit. But it added to the nervousness that surfaced when I arrived in my home town.

As I started to visit my mother more regularly, my brother's three daughters often showed up right away happy to see me. Their mother would visit during my stay, but in the beginning my brother, my only sibling, refused to come into my mother's house if I was there. Over the years, this changed, he visited me at my mother's, and I was even invited to his home.

One summer when I was studying for the Bar Exam for my license as an attorney, my daughters went to stay with Ben's family for awhile. The girls, who were about six years old, also spent some time at my mother's and were welcomed as well to visit my brother's home. This allowed the five girl cousins to get to know each other. I give my brother credit for the growth he showed over the years.

Over the years I sometimes visited my mother with the girls and sometimes on my own. From the beginning, my mother was able to be kind and caring with my daughters, and she and I were comfortable with a polite, congenial relationship. I remember proposing to her early on that discussions about politics, religion and race not be part of our communication, and she agreed. Although I did not intend that to mean we could not discuss the history of our relationship, we never had a direct discussion about how our differences and our feelings had affected us and our relationship. But occasionally she would make a point of telling me how nice the Black woman was who delivered her mail or how her church was doing some kind of joint project with a Black church. I knew she wanted me to know she was growing in her understanding, and I appreciated it.

On these trips I would always visit Ben's mom. We would often go out to lunch together. She always chose places where she knew she was welcome, and that she felt we would be welcomed together. So we never had any difficulties. We may have gotten some stares, but nothing more.

I invited my mother to visit me and the girls in California. She made numerous trips over the years. Sometimes she came alone, and other times she traveled with one of her granddaughters or her sister who sometimes was accompanied by one or two of her daughters.

Through visits to see my mother or her visits to California, I began to feel that I, my daughters and our lives could be seen as more normal and acceptable than my mother and others might have imagined. My daughters were very open and happy to have time with our family. I give them credit for helping to ease this reconnecting with family. They were warm and accepting and encouraged those feelings in all of us.

Nevertheless, for a long time I held on to some feeling that I was still being judged and condemned, particularly by many of the extended family. I often felt that I couldn't entirely be myself.

Gradually, I had more contact with more extended family members, including invitations to lunch or dinner. I felt there was more tolerance, if not acceptance. I saw signs in the community that there was more racial mixing than when I lived there. It was almost always something of a surprise when I was not met with coldness or rejection. I wanted to believe that people's minds could open. I was grateful to be treated cordially, but I still often felt anxious.

I was relieved to feel that some changes had occurred in the South. I witnessed how my mother and my brother had made amazing shifts in their openness and acceptance. My mother moved from total fear and rejection into willingness to welcome us and accept an experience of family that had seemed impossible. And I must acknowledge that was not something many people could do.

In 2004 my mother was living alone at age 84. She was very healthy and independent. She rarely saw a doctor. The genes on her side of the family supported our belief that she had many years of health ahead. Her 92 year old sister and her 98 year old brother lived alone in their homes where they had spent all their adult years.

On the day I returned to Maui in September, 2004 after a visit with my mother, she had a serious fall. She was exercising the physical strength and independence she possessed. She was moving some furniture in the guest bedroom in order to replace some weak flooring she had discovered. Her leg went through the floor, breaking her femur in three places. She managed to get her leg out, but she couldn't reach a phone. She was found by her oldest granddaughter about 24 hours later dehydrated and in shock. She had surgery to put pins in her leg, and her generally excellent health helped with her recovery from surgery.

I arrived to care for her during her rehabilitation on the day she was transferred to the rehab hospital in early October. From there she had to continue inpatient rehab at a skilled nursing facility, where she moved in November. My role during that period was to visit her daily and to encourage her to do the work needed to walk again. Physically, she made good progress, but the trauma of her fall seemed to have had a strong impact on her will to live — to recover.

I set a goal for her to go home by Christmas Eve, which she seemed to be encouraged by. As that date approached, her doctor agreed she could go home on that date and start outpatient rehab in January.

Once at home she was often resistant to moving forward and insisted she couldn't do new tasks. She seemed to believe she was less capable than she was, but by March she was walking well with a walker and doing basic self-care. A plan was worked out with her, my brother, my niece and me to allow her to be at home. She was strongly opposed to leaving her home or to having part time or live in assistance. My brother and my niece would help her with anything that she could not do for herself, and I was to return to my home. We all believed that once I left she would have more incentive to take care of herself and resume her independent life. After a few weeks, in April she spent a short time in the hospital and was then sent to assisted living. After a week in assisted living, we learned she had contacted sepsis, perhaps while in the hospital. She was sent back in the hospital and her organs were shutting down. When I arrived she seemed to be in and out of consciousness. I spent the night at the hospital and talked to her off and on all night. She passed the next morning, when one of my daughters, my oldest niece, my brother and I were present. She seemed to finally relax, and her breathing stopped.

My other daughter arrived later that day. My family and my brother's family gathered at her home to jointly take care of all the arrangements for her funeral and other details. That gathering, although sad, felt like the company of family, supporting each other in harmony. The funeral with extended family, including my daughters and Ben's mother was an extension of that feeling. Everyone who approached me, even those who I hadn't seen for thirty-five years, was open and caring.

That evening after the funeral when I was having dinner with my daughter, I remember making a promise to myself: "I'm not coming back here until I can truly be myself." I was aware that it was still hard for me to relax and be myself in that environment, because there was often a feeling that under the surface, some, not everyone, could not get over their rejection. I felt I had to be guarded and careful to do what would gain approval. I didn't want to feel that way. I wanted to let go of needing to prove myself.

Ten years later the girls and I got wedding invitations from my brother's granddaughter. She had been twelve when I last saw her. She wanted all of us to come for her wedding. I had to ask myself if I was ready to return, and I wasn't sure.

One of my daughters wanted to go. She wanted to bring her husband and her child (P) and have them meet that side of her family and see the place where both of her parents were born and raised. My daughter wanted me to go with them. I wanted to be there for my great-niece. I wanted to see members of my family who I was closest to. I decided to go.

I was thinking a lot about the promise to myself that I had to be able to be my true self. At the same time I had some concerns about how we as a group might be treated. The location of the wedding was the largest Baptist church in town. I felt proud of my great niece for sincerely wanting us to be there. I expected my family to be the only Black people to attend. My son-in-law is a large, African man from the Democratic Republic of the Congo. He was granted asylum in the United States after coming to the U.S. to go to college, and he is now a U.S. citizen. My grandchild (P) was adopted by my daughter when she was single and later by her husband. P is the grandchild you met in the Introduction to this story.

None of my white family members had met my son-in-law and P. I had anxiety about what could happen in that town or in the country outside of town. When my cousin heard we were coming, she and her two sisters invited us to come to lunch the day before the wedding. They all had houses on the old family farm that belonged to their parents and before that to our grandparents. I knew a bit about the history of the small town near the farm. It was historically a sundown town — a town that prohibited Black people from being there after sunset. The thought of the four of us going there made me very nervous. I knew the anxiety was based on my associations with the past, and that I wouldn't agree to go if I seriously thought there was danger. I accepted the invitation.

Before the trip, I woke up in the middle of the night two nights in a row in a deep state of fear, which was unusual for me. I felt strongly that I had to face the fear and stay with it. This was very difficult and painful. Both nights the fear subsided after some period of time. I have no clear sense of how long it took. The morning after the second night I had no anxiety, and I had no more fear in the following nights. I became excited about the trip and completely at ease. That state of ease continued for the entire trip and beyond. I had no worry of harm and no worry about what anyone thought about me. I felt free to be myself. I felt free of the sense of condemnation toward me that I had so long carried. The feeling that I wouldn't be accepted wasn't there, because it didn't matter! It was a state of Grace — a healing.

When we arrived at my cousin's home, I felt embraced in genuine caring and openness both from my cousins and within myself. We left there to go to my niece's home where the wedding preparation was happening. It was for me the same experience. It was a sincere and loving welcome. I saw my great-niece, the bride, as an adult for the first time and met other great-nieces for the first time. P had a good time meeting all of the many girl cousins.

The wedding and reception the next day were beautiful and fun. There were only two people who I felt were cold toward me. It didn't affect me. I knew it was not my problem. I was relaxed and happy that we were there.

PART 4

WORKING TOWARD BEING AN ALLY

I am writing from the perspective of a white person raised in the South with certain assumptions about segregation and distinctions based on skin color. That was my starting point. How did I come to question this deeply ingrained position? I mentioned earlier the recognition of the hypocrisy I saw in the church members' acceptance of treating other humans as inferior and unworthy, contrary to the teachings of Jesus who they professed to follow. I know that made a deep impression on me and who I wanted to be.

Another impression was made by my maternal grand-mother with whom I spent a lot of time as a child. My family lived with my grandparents when I was born until I was four. My grandmother was like a second mother. She never spoke to me specifically about racism, but I remember that she often expressed to me that it was important never to think you are better than anyone else. I think it was a very important lesson, which I try to live by.

My approach to working to be an ally supporting the equality of all, as promised (but ignored) in the founding of our country, begins with each of us looking into our hearts and heads recognizing the beliefs we are taught directly or indirectly, examining what we feel and what we question. This is part of the growth required to be fully humane and whole individuals.

What is the need to feel superior? Are we willing to examine that need in ourselves and in others, remembering that finding the desire to be free of it starts the change. It won't be instant. Being completely free of all forms of racism is essentially impossible in the world of deeply entrenched ideas, beliefs and stereotypes. That's why the next step beyond caring about equality and believing in a fair playing field is to educate ourselves about the history that has been hidden, denied or ignored, and to learn about the motivations to create laws and systems to keep the separation and inequity.

Doing our own personal work to examine where we are includes being willing to own the ways in which our heads hold on to biases that would be hard to admit. We are part of a culture that accepts stereotypes, consciously or unconsciously, takes for granted our privileges, and feels that we have no need to work to eliminate unequal treatment of people of color. We all, no matter our race, our upbringing, our education or our intentions, carry, to some degree, the fallout of living in a world with the deeply imbedded need to categorize human beings and their value based upon our biases. Stereotyping individuals in a particular group as having all the traits identified, rightly or erroneously, with that group is one of the most common forms of prejudice and hardest to be free of.

Recognizing our own racial biases, admitting them and working not to live by them takes one a long way toward being an ally. This is often a very hard thing for people to do, but it is our work if we are committed. Many of us are unwilling to admit even to ourselves that we hold racial bias. We equate it with being bad, and we think of ourselves as good people with good intentions. It is not bad to recognize that we have been taught by the society we are part of to think a certain way, but it is only up to each of us to discern what is the truth.

I am listing below some of the commonly discussed suggestions that help us move toward being an ally. There are many sources on-line with suggestions for "how to work to be an ally."

HOW TO WORK TO BE AN ALLY FOR BLACK, INDIGENOUS PEOPLE OF COLOR (BIPOC)

1. Do a personal assessment of where you are with your own bias. Recognize that we all have some bias and admit to yourself and others how it shows up.

2. Educate yourself from reliable sources about the history of racism in our country and around the world. Read or view Black accounts of slavery, Reconstruction, Jim Crow Laws, the struggle for Civil Rights and Voting Rights, and the effect of mass incarceration. Read fiction by Black authors that helps you understand more diversified views of Black culture (not just what is shown on popular culture television and movies.)

3. Be aware that things you say or do with no negative intent can be hurtful and disrespectful. Accept that it is the impact of what you do or say, not the intent that matters. Through educating yourself and making Black friends you will learn more and more about what is offensive. Apologize. Don't defend by saying "I didn't intend . . ." or try to explain unless asked. Show your willingness to learn.

4. In a diverse or mostly white group or meeting, when discussion is appropriate, allow everyone the opportunity to speak by encouraging different perspectives.

5. Remember your role is one of support. It is not to put yourself in the center or try to control. Think of yourself as continually learning how to be an ally. It is not for you to determine when you are recognized as an ally. Keep in mind that some white people are very comfortable asserting themselves, speaking over or for others, speaking with authority and announcing their expertise, which can be controlling and resented. Be mindful of your support role, but be ready to offer your skills and privileged access when needed.

6. Learn to speak up when you see or hear racist acts or words. It takes courage, especially in a group where you may be the only one objecting. It is important to raise consciousness about racist behavior. You can learn how to speak calmly and directly, such as, "That's offensive and unnecessary." You can press the point with comments like: "What do you mean?"; "What do you base that on?"; "It surprises me to hear you talk like that." When you find it difficult to find what to say, you can start with "Ouch. That hurt." And continue with why it hurt.

Calling out racist words or actions is one of the most important things an ally can do. Sometimes it's hard to react immediately. You may need time to think about how to address the offensive word or action or you may feel you need to pre-pare yourself.

I experienced a situation with a woman in my home when we were discussing movies. She was telling me about seeing the film "12 Years a Slave." She was criticizing it, saying it was way over the top with all the outrageous violence and mistreatment. She said that she and her husband had decided it was a film made to make white people feel guilty. I couldn't believe those words came from her. She is a politically progressive woman, well educated and I had never heard her say anything racially offensive. I sat there not knowing what to say. I had not seen the movie yet, but I'm sure my face must have shown my disbelief. I'm sorry I said nothing at the time, but I immediately told myself that I would talk to her after I saw the movie. I knew the movie was based on a true story, and I wanted to see it. Now I knew I had to see it.

The next time I saw her I said, "We need to talk." I told her how surprised I was to hear her comment about the movie, and that I didn't know what to say at the time. Mentioning that it was based on a true story, I said that it was a powerful story and true to what I understand about slavery, and that it was painful to think she believed that the intent of a movie about slavery was about guilt. I expressed that I've never known Black people to have an agenda to make white people feel guilty. What I see is their wanting understanding and recognition of what they and their ancestors have experienced. They want their history known and not denied. They want to be seen and treated with respect as human beings entitled to equality and justice.

She received what I told her, and did not get defensive. She seemed to appreciate it, and said she had not understood why the movie was created. My impression was that she was considering what I expressed.

We cannot always expect to be heard when we speak up, but we may be heard, and we may not always know. All we can do is speak from our hearts.

PART 5

ETTIE LYNN: MY INSPIRATION

A Related Short Story

Ettie Minerva Callahan Lynn taught me, not by the rules she made, but by being herself in my company. She was my maternal grandmother, known as "Mama" to all in her family. I was the tenth of her eleven grandchildren and the first child of her baby girl.

Mama was safe harbor and a live spark in my young, constrained world. While my mother was consumed with whether I might misbehave, and my dad seemed to seldom notice my presence, Mama simply enjoyed having me around.

"You're Mama's favorite," complained my cousin, Nancy, who was four years older than me and Mama's ninth grandchild.

"You get time alone with her. You even got to live with her," she continued. It was true. At the time of her marriage in 1946 my mother, the last of four children, lived in her parents' home. After the wedding my dad moved in, and they lived in the back bedroom for more than five years. During those years they saved enough money to buy their own place, and they produced two children. I was born eight days before their first anniversary, and my brother was born eight days before my first birthday.

During my first year I may have thought I had two mothers, but my brother's arrival upset that notion. As I turned one and my mother's attention was on the new baby, I became my grandmother's baby. Our move from her home when I was four must have been difficult for both of us.

My parents' new house, a simple, post-World War II, five-room, wooden bungalow, was less than two miles from my grandparents. I was the most frequent visitor to my grandparents' home on and was the only grandchild with overnight privileges.

My grandparents were farmers most of their lives. Papa supplemented their farming income as a salesman of the products of Dr. Watkins. As they aged the hope of an easier life led them to sell the farm to my aunt and uncle. They bought the Jackson Street house and moved into town a few years before I was born.

Papa was a tall, slim man with large nose and rough complexion. Seeing him in his suspendered pants and white shirt, I saw an aged Abraham Lincoln.

Mama was a foot shorter than Papa, and she was full of figure. Her kind eyes were the striking feature of her round face. Her gray hair was short and permed, and she always wore simple, but colorful, floral shirtwaist dresses.

My first memory that was unquestionably my own, not confused with what I imagined upon hearing someone's story or seeing old photographs, was an eventful day with my grandparents when I was six. My first and last real memory of Papa was his death. My grandfather was not a healthy man, but the family had not expected that death was imminent. Certainly I hadn't. I had spent the night with them, and I was sitting with Papa on the screened back porch while Mama worked near-by in the kitchen.

"Sharon, go find my green tin can. I need it."

I searched the house and found the canister in the kitchen. I returned to the porch and saw Papa lying on the floor next to his chair. I gasped and managed a small scream, "Papa!" He did not answer or move. I dropped the canister and ran to the kitchen to find my grandmother.

It happened so fast. He was gone. He spoke his last words to me. As I reflect on what happened years ago, I wonder, "Did he know that he needed to send me out of the room? Did he know what was coming?"

What happened after I found him and during the next few days is mostly a blur. I remember seeing the open casket in the living room and at the church, seeing Papa as if he were sleeping, but knowing this was different. I wondered why I wasn't crying like ten-year-old Nancy. Wasn't I the one who knew him? Why didn't I understand?

After Papa's passing in the summer of 1953, my grandmother and I found mutual comfort in our time together. I started school for the first time that year. Going to Mama's house to eat supper and spend the night after a week at school became a regular Friday event for me.

Although Mama was never regarded in the family as a great cook, there were dishes she made that were outstanding to me. She never fit the perfect housekeeper and cook image. What she chose to cook she did well. What I remember are specific dishes, not well-organized family meals. I recall her homemade mac and cheese, corn bread made in a fry pan, chicken and dumplings (like no one else could make), pecan pie and a dessert called snow pie, which was a very light custard-like filling in a pie crust. At Christmas she made jam cake filled with walnuts, dry fruit and apparently jam.

When anyone was sick she made what she called gruel, a surprisingly tasty flour-based soup that was the ultimate comfort food. Sometimes she and I made a meal of her corn bread crumbled into buttermilk -- an acquired taste, yet it became such a simple treat.

Much of my fondness for genuine Southern cooking has been ignored as an adult who moved west. Trying to be more calorie-conscious and, perhaps, more sophisticated, I developed what I thought was a more gourmet palette. But what could be more gourmet than Mama's fresh-from-the- garden, young mustard greens salad with tender green onions, crisp crumbled bacon, and hot bacon grease drizzled over the top.

On Friday nights Mama and I cooked our favorite foods or experimented, devising tasty new concoctions. When neither of us had heard of taco salad, we created our own version that we called hamburger salad -- lettuce (probably iceberg), chopped tomatoes, onions and crumbled ground beef. We had never seen an avocado, but I know she would have loved the addition of guacamole to this salad that we enjoyed regularly and thought was so unique.

When we cooked we talked. I was a very shy child, but with her I was at home. I talked without the usual caution and concern of misstep. I listened to her stories and life lessons.

"When you were eighteen months old I sat up night after night, rocking you and holding you upright so you could breathe."

"I couldn't breathe. How come?"

"Swollen tonsils. "Finally the doctor decided that your tonsils and adenoids had to go. Never heard of that in one so little, but you got better, and we both got some sleep."

"Were you the only one who stayed up with me?"

"Sure. Your mother had a new baby and needed all the sleep she could get."

She seemed to cherish her role as my comforter, and I accepted my good fortune. Not every child has her own "mother" when the new baby shows up. I was lucky that I had a grandmother who was my Mama.

In our family and community Mama would not have been labeled an eccentric or misfit, but in our conservative environment she was something of an individual. She made her own standards for housecleaning. She seemed to have no strong inner critic running her daily life. Unlike the rest of the extended family, she did not attend church regularly. She read her Bible often, taught me what she felt were the important Christian values, but she was quite happy in her rocking chair viewing church service on television. She had her favorite preachers, and she could control the on and off button at her discretion. No one else I knew did that. For a long time I thought her age gave her that option. I learned that it was her willingness to defy convention in what seemed to be small ways, but ways that showed her inclination to do things her way.

I don't know how objective my view was of her character, but to me she was a generous, caring person. Not everyone saw her as I did.

"She can be a stubborn one at times," said her neighbor, Willa.

"She certainly has her opinions," my mother liked to point out.

If she was stubborn and opinionated, it didn't bother me. I knew her as the one who taught me about respect for everyone. Her favorite lesson, or the one I remember most clearly, was about equality. She taught me passionately not to think I was better than others and never to mistreat anyone, because they had less than me.

"You're not better than anyone, and no one is better than you," she told me regularly. I don't remember that she ever talked to me about this in the context of racism, though we lived in a highly segregated world. I can't recall or imagine anything that suggested that not mistreating others meant other white people.

In 2004 I had the opportunity to hear a talk by The Dalai Lama. I heard him speak that same message. It seems so simple, but how many children are taught that having self-esteem includes accepting equality.

If Mama had known about self-esteem, she would have said, "If you have real self-esteem, you don't need to think you're special." Mama would have been in agreement with The Dalai Lama. (Inspired by that message, in 2005 I wrote a children's story entitled "Better Than Everybody Else?")

As I grew older Mama and I were close, but my overnight visits were less frequent. I became a teenager, busy with friends. Then as a college student I was away from home, and she adapted, just as parents do, to the empty nest.

My love for her was always strong. However, I went through a period of neglectfulness, characteristic of a young adult needing to assert her independence.

While I was away at college, she fell at home, broke her hip, and moved to a nursing home. I visited her there when I was in town and after college more frequently, but certainly not as often as she would have liked. I knew she was unhappy not to be at home. What could I do? I had to begin my life. It was a very turbulent time for me.

Almost two years after college I moved away, and I never explained to her that I was leaving or why. My parents discouraged me from sharing with her what was happening. They told me that I would break her heart. I'm sure they believed that. I was afraid that they were right. I'm sure I broke her heart, because I disappeared, and no one ever told her why.

My deepest regret is that I left her like that. I don't regret my life choices, that I moved to California with the Black man who I married against the conventional rules in Arkansas in 1971. Even though I was rejected for years by most of my family, my only regret was not saying "goodbye" to Mama.

She died in the nursing home, and the call came to me in California too late to allow me to attend the funeral. I'm not sure I would have gone to the funeral. I wish I had gone before she passed.

EPILOGUE

PART 1 : HUMAN BEINGS CANNOT BE PROPERTY

In 2019 Nicole Hannah-Jones produced The 1619 Project as a magazine for the New York Times, marking the 400th anniversary of the arrival of the first ship of enslaved people to America. It is a remarkable story of the mistreatment of enslaved people and their descendants. It provides many details and events that have been essentially deleted from the history we have been taught.

Many of us missed this outstanding publication in 2019. It came to my attention after the murder of George Floyd in 2020, when so many young, talented experts, speaking about the history of slavery and systemic racism still surviving in American institutions, were appearing on numerous television talk shows. When I heard Nicole Hannah-Jones being interviewed in 2020, I was impressed with the depth of her knowledge on these issues. I researched The 1619 Project Magazine, and I borrowed a copy from a friend who had read and preserved it in 2019.

In the first essay in the 1619 Project, Hannah-Jones describes the arrival of this ship into the newly established English colonies in North America. It arrived in Virginia in 1619 with between 20 and 30 African people. Plantation owners in Virginia paid the traders for human beings and began a system in America of treating these people as chattel, controlling every aspect of their lives and profiting from their uncompensated labor.

Then came the arrival of more ships and more auctions of men, women and children — 250 years of degradation. This was followed by years of what was called "freedom," a period marked by the creation of laws, customs and beliefs that were specifically aimed at preventing the advancement of the formerly enslaved and their descendants.

What slave trader or plantation owner or government or king or queen or any other human being has the authority to steal one's humanity for their own personal gain or any other reason? How could anyone ever legally or morally own another human being? These questions kept coming back to me. I started to formulate in my mind how the ownership of humans has no legitimacy.

One day I finally put pen to paper and put the various thoughts together in the following "formula."

HUMAN BEINGS CANNOT BE PROPERTY

NO RIGHT TO OWN ANOTHER HUMAN BEING =

NO VALID CONTRACT TO BUY OR SELL HUMANS BECAUSE THE SELLER HAS NO OWNERSHIP =

NO OWNERSHIP BY A BUYER IF THERE IS NO VALID CONTRACT =

NO OWNERSHIP = NO FREE LABOR = THEFT = DEBT OWED

This formula was created in the form of a legal analysis. The question raised is both a legal and a moral question. The formula is helpful to see that those who purchased humans at any point in time had no legal right of ownership. Legally speaking, paying money for property that the seller does not own does not make one an owner, and no piece of paper changes that. As I looked further into the issue I came to see more clearly that it is not just a legal and moral matter, it is an issue of the innate, inherent nature of humanity. As human beings, we are all born with intrinsic, inalienable rights. We are sentient beings. We cannot be property. We are not objects or things, but living human beings.

What or who could authorize or entitle one to own another human life? No one! It is a major and unforgivable fallacy that people were ever property that could be legally owned.

PART 2 : WHAT NEEDS TO BE SEEN

When I first read about the arrival of the first slave ship in what was to become our country, it caused me to think more deeply about this occurrence that has had such a major impact on our country, its history and the lives of so many souls. How often do we hear references to slavery, and we don't give much thought or feeling to what it means?

It existed in many parts of the world before it came to this continent, but why did a group of land owners in Virginia allow the thought that humans could become chattel forever with no rights to govern their own lives. How did this thinking begin a horrendous injustice in a country, which held out the establishment of freedom as its cornerstone? How could so many for so long accept that this was an acceptable practice?

Doesn't it make you wonder how so many "good" people both then and today do not in their own hearts know the evil of what was done and that the consequences of that evil have never been repaired. When they say "That's the past, we are not responsible" are they unable to see that we as a country still owe a great debt?

Those who lived in slavery can never be paid for what was taken from them. Those who lived in the years after the Civil War, during Jim Crow laws and into the days of the lasting systemic racism of the institutions of this country continue to be the recipients of what happened to their ancestors.

This is still true today for people of African descent, indigenous people and many other people of color, because they are so often not fully seen and accepted as full human beings, entitled to respect and treatment as full human beings. If you do not know this, you have not opened your eyes and been willing to see the truth of what is before you, or you choose to live a life very sheltered from all but the very privileged world.

WHAT needs to be SEEN in order to repair this outrageous error of OUR history? First the tragedy of the inhumanity must be recognized and ownership taken for what was allowed in this country. Many can see only what the South "lost," and are unable to let themselves see the hundreds of years of real suffering created and perpetuated upon the innocent human beings taken from their homeland to become property. Many cannot see the obstacles created to prevent the descendants of the enslaved from achieving real freedom.

Do we teach our children that when they make a mistake they should deny the truth and try to cover it up? Not if we care about being a people of integrity and character. As a country, we made many mistakes that began with slavery and grew out of a belief that equality was not really deserved by all, contrary to what we professed as the foundation of our country.

Besides seeing the truth about our failures, what is needed today to help correct the consequences of these failures?

I was recently saw a photograph of my grandson and three other young Black men standing with backpacks on the first day of school. Two are entering high school for the first time. The other two are seniors. I zoomed into a close up of those beautiful faces. How deeply I hope for their dreams to be available and fulfilled, for their lives at this time to be troubled only with the inevitable teenage worries. I pray for a time soon when their lives can be free from stereotypes based on their skin color, which do not take into account the individual human beings they are.

Stereotyping is often a distorted and harmful generalization applied to members of a group without regard to the history, experience, character or innocence of the individuals within that group. Young Black men are often stereotyped and feared as criminals. This is the source of much of the difficulty causing fear in those who automatically react to every unknown Black man with suspicion and concerns for safety. This stereotyping or a similar version, causing automatic suspicion, is also the source of the perpetual fear and anxiety carried by Black people in many of their movements through life. For many young Black men this fear is intensified in any interaction with police, often causing them to resist or feel they must run or fight for their lives.

Stereotypes are often based on something that is true of some group members, but cannot accurately be applied to all or even most. Some young Black men do turn to crime, but that is not because they are Black. This statement defies the conclusion that many uninformed individuals assume. There are many factors and obstacles that determine the reasons for committing crime. This is not to excuse that choice. It is to say it is not about race. We know crime is committed by all types of people. The fact that certain groups may have a higher crime rate has more to do with the disparity of opportunities and choices they have, rather than to what group they are born into. Most of us actually know this logically, but it is sometimes easier to jump over logic to our preconceived ideas.

What can we do about this kind of thinking that can be harmful to ourselves and others? First, we can recognize when these kinds of reactions arise and remember they come from beliefs, and as a generalization they are unfair, not likely to be true, and they are the core of much of the discomfort between groups who make assumptions about the other and are unable to see individuals as they are.

It is not easy to free our minds of stereotypes. Recognizing when you are falling into a stereotype is the first step. Don't deny to yourself or others that it is happening. Own the fact that it is there and that you understand that it is simply an idea that you have learned. Finally, practice trying to see the truth of the situation.

Everyone of all races and cultures learns stereotypes of all kinds. You can practice seeing the kinds of stereotypes you hold and practice acknowledging them and being willing to see individuals and their truth.

PART 3: TRUE CHANGE —
HEALING HATEFUL BELIEFS

Some of the necessary components for living the dream of the ancestors who never had a true life of their own in this country include:

1. Access to opportunities to get the required education, training and experience to be successful;

2. The changes that reflect that one has a fair chance without expecting to be treated as unworthy;

3. Changes in attitudes and actions that sustain racism with disrespect and indifference, seeing only skin color.

4. The freedom from fear and ever present vigilance, particularly that affecting the lives of young Black men.

I never set out to write an argument for reparations. It just showed up. First, I want to point out that reparations are not just about money. From the list above, you will note that most of the items listed aren't about something that can be bought. They require changes in the way we think and see. Only then can true change happen. That is not to say that we can't work now to begin the necessary corrections. It is to say that the necessary changes in our attitudes and beliefs are essential, and this is a lot of what we as individuals can do.

Some would say that hearts and minds are not likely to change. I agree that there are those who will not change, but I have seen changes in deep seated beliefs and attitudes in my own family and particularly in young people. Often it requires opening to new experiences and interactions.

Since the murder of George Floyd in 2020, there have been shifts in the understanding of many white people and more exposure to the truth of the Black experience. There has also been backlash against telling the truth about the past and the current consequences of racial hatred and violence. The denial of our country's history has been amplified in the actions to ban books and lessons that expose students to the history of slavery and racism, claiming they make white children feel bad about being white. Advocates of those bans try to stamp out the role of teaching factual history and the importance of learning respect and equal treatment for those who are not the same as them. The denial of the truth and these bans are a major obstacle for many young people learning about this country's role in committing crimes against humanity that have not been repaid.

On the other hand, could the denial of the truth that is being exposed backfire with students being curious and maybe outraged at what is being covered up? A new rebel generation could be created! Regardless of that possibility, education curriculum teaching accurate depictions of slavery, racism and their consequences, as well as, the history and contributions of Black, indigenous and other people of color should be more than minor lessons in our schools. Requiring and encouraging this curriculum in schools is an essential component in educating young people with the material that has been largely missing. A meaningful education about this part of our history could mean a crucial change in the harmful attitudes and actions of bias, hatred, superiority, disrespect, indifference and violence.

Calls for reparations for slavery and its consequences have been presented for years in the United States with no significant response. Laws have been passed prohibiting discrimination, resolutions passed and executive orders issued for changes in federal government practices and policies, but impactful reparation plans and bills have been ignored and rejected.

Reparations take many forms, and they include, but are not limited to; truth-seeking and acknowledgment of the wrongs perpetuated, formal apologies; memorialization; compensation; examining and altering policing and the systems of justice including prison reform; improving education opportunities; correcting the barriers to housing access; assuring that ACCURATE AND COMPREHENSIVE DEPICTIONS OF HISTORY are taught in schools alongside encouragement for respect and tolerance for differences.

I would add that attitudes and beliefs that sustain racism need a deep, honest investigation to facilitate understanding and how to address the factors that impede healing, leading us to a path of true repair and recovery.

Finally, I would also ask the radical questions: Is racial hatred/white supremacy only a moral issue? Could it be considered a psychological condition to hold deep hatred — not as something to be used against someone or to excuse someone, but to be studied and treated?